By Chance

By Chance

Poems by

Emily H. Axelrod

© 2023 Emily H. Axelrod. All rights reserved.
This material may not be reproduced in any form, published,
reprinted, recorded, performed, broadcast,
rewritten or redistributed without
the explicit permission of Emily H. Axelrod.
All such actions are strictly prohibited by law.

Cover design by Shay Culligan
Cover image by Emily H. Axelrod, "Magic Door in Samland"

ISBN: 978-1-63980-282-1

Kelsay Books
502 South 1040 East, A-119
American Fork, Utah 84003
Kelsaybooks.com

In memory of Ashley Bryan,
inspiration, guiding spirit, and beloved friend.

Acknowledgments

I have been fortunate to work for many years with a small group of inspired poets and a gifted teacher. Thank you Katia Kapovich, writer, award-winning poet, editor of *Fulcrum, An Annual of Poetry and Aesthetics,* for everything you have taught me. Thanks also to the MIT Poetry Workshop, talented poets whose insights and support have been invaluable. Cambridge poet Alec Solomita, (*Hard to Be a Hero,* Kelsay Books, 2022), has generously contributed his superb editing skills to this volume. And finally, no acknowledgement would be complete without thanking my friends and family—I couldn't do it without you.

Contents

I.

My Grandmother's House   15
Piano Lessons   16
Rope Swing   17
Driving Lessons   18
Second Love   19
Satin Ribbon   20

II.

Motherhood   23
Recipe Cards   24
Ironing   25
A Daughter's Visit   26
Across the Water   27
Driving to Charlestown   28
Ferry   29
Moontree   30
Sprite   31
Atticus   32
When My Husband Goes Away II   33
Fine China   34
Then and Now   35
Golden Years   36

III.

COVID Days   39
This April   40
By Chance   41
Quarantine   42
Birds   43
Love Story   44

IV.

Morning Light	47
Two Poems	48
Night Swim	49
A Thousand Words	50
Faith	51
Red Line	52
Matinee	53
Drinking	54
Cardinal	55
Graveside	56
Mountain Lake	57
At the Dock	58
Fog	59
Roses	60
Summer's End	61

I.

My Grandmother's House

for Nancy

My sister and I
caught lizards in a shoebox
and fed them lettuce
from the Sunday table.
We slept in twin beds
between sheets as cold as ice,
with down pillows and silken quilts
that slid to the floor.
Our grandmother did the mending
in a chair facing Mt. Tamalpais,
while the dozing lizards
lay silent in their narrow house.
After the stroke
the nurses let her grey hair
fall to her shoulders,
and held it back
with a wide pink ribbon.
She looked like a young girl
ready for the ball.

Piano Lessons

The black Steinway baby grand
promised full, sweet notes
to fill our quiet house with music.
Its mammoth sounding board
was painted gold, and above
the ivory keyboard
its black finish was dull and cracked
from too many years at the window,
absorbing the western sun.

Each week I practiced,
my feet just reaching the pedals,
wishing I loved to play,
if only to please the kind man
who came on Wednesday afternoons
to teach me, forever a novice
plucking distractedly at the polished keys.
He must have hoped that one afternoon
I would breathe life into the piano,
finding the sonorous notes and perfect chords
it was meant to proclaim.

Instead, I memorized *Für Elise*
and played without feeling,
working out stunted melodies
to the tick of the metronome,
gazing at the city beyond.

Rope Swing

We looped a rope over a branch
and swung high above a hospital
where inpatients paced
on porches caged in wire.
One young man watched us
every afternoon,
and when he stopped appearing
we wondered where he had gone.

Driving Lessons

You taught me to drive the Chevy
in a clearing near the gravel pit,
and on the hills of San Francisco.
From you I learned the beauty
of a flawless downshift
and a smooth start
at the crest of a hill.
And from you I learned to dread
the coming of the cocktail hour.
An imperfect romance,
a girl and her father,
a fitting rehearsal
for all that life would bring.

Second Love

It was my second love
who mattered most,
dark-haired boy, soulful and sad.
We explored the terrain of love,
from steamy nights on coastal sands
to wintry days in redwood groves
where we walked among trees
as tall as mountains.
Touch was our guide
as we read each other's bodies
to the sound of fog
dripping a steady patter
on our cabin roof.
In the end it was words,
jagged and unforgiving,
that broke like a rogue wave
sending us to distant lives
far from the small house
in the trees.

Satin Ribbon

We sifted through
the trappings of their life,
readying the house
for strangers.
In the bedroom,
clothing for Goodwill,
outdated ledgers,
calendars with days gone by
and dented silver bracelets
we passed on
to our daughters.

In my mother's closet
a bundle of letters
from the war years,
wrapped with satin ribbon
and filled with endearments.
I began to read the brittle pages,
but soon replaced the ribbon,
tying it just as before.
Now the letters sit in my closet,
the satin ribbon faded by time,
safeguarding their wartime romance.

II.

Motherhood

For David and Melissa

You were so small,
how could I understand
that the years would disappear
one snowstorm at a time,
and with each blooming of the apple tree.

Wasn't it yesterday or this morning
that world of snow days and blanket tents,
of sleepovers and birthday candles
when we moved to rhythms
that only we could know.

Climbing the stairs each night,
inhaling the scent of your innocence,
I was free to dream
of lives that know no harm.

Then your first broken heart
became my own, and the memory
of a hospital waiting room
left scars deep in my bones
that ache still in cold winter air.

You move now in circles
beyond my creation,
shaped by all we shared
and all that you
have come to love.

Recipe Cards

I open the battered box,
moved by the sight
of my mother's loopy script
on index cards, some stained,
others barely legible.
Leafing through family recipes,
memories unwind
like movie reels,
brittle on their spools.
Macaroni and cheese
in the brown glazed pot,
roast chicken forever paired
with a stormy departure
from the dinner table.
I choose the same recipes
year after year,
bent on creating evenings
free from dread,
the battered paper
rough and familiar,
their texture and smell
redolent with memory.

Ironing

I iron the way my mother taught me,
wrinkled cotton dampened
then wrung into coils
waiting for the steaming iron
to flatten creases
and lift the smell of clean cotton
into the air.
Standing at the ironing board
I think of her
and those labors of love,
arranging his ironed shirts
on wooden hangers,
over and over again.

A Daughter's Visit

When she leaves
petals are falling
from the small bouquet
I had placed next to her bed.
I gather the sheets and towels
remembering the child
asleep in her cozy berth,
soft cocoon of home.
She has returned
to her separate life,
a shifting landscape filled
with unanswered questions,
and I ache for the easy intimacy
and gatherings at the table,
struggling once more
with letting go.

Across the Water

We visited your classroom
where you had drawn the continents
in colored chalk on the blackboard,
and listed the spelling word of the day.
Plants overran the windowsill
and a tangle of boots and jackets
filled the hall. We sat in child-sized chairs
and listened from the back row,
proud and amazed.

On the day we left,
we looked back across the water
from the stern of the ferry.
A strip of light emerged
on the surface of the Sound
and we knew the sun would
soon light up your house
on the distant shore.

Driving to Charlestown

The river throws the morning sun
on brick facades, red and ochre shades
of New England clay.
At my daughter's house
I take the baby in my arms
and stroke his small head
as he falls into sleep.
The day is his, illuminated
by the same sun, but here
there is only the moment.
On the drive home
the river is dark and quiet,
the skyline a static silhouette
against the falling light.
The river flows
with no measure of time
while I mark my days
with each small milestone
of new life.

Ferry

From the picture window we could see
the ferry leaving the terminal
beginning its weekly trip to Alaska,
smokestacks streaming dark plumes
into the saturated sky,
hulking prow steady in the winter chop.

You watched as the grey sky
and unrelenting rain
pushed you deeper into thought
knowing that your life was gaining steam
like the great churning engines of the ferry,
but with no charted course.

Together we searched the horizon
for a break in the clouds
that might deliver a glint of light,
but on that day the rain persisted
and the silhouette of the ferry
moved slowly out of sight.

Moontree

for Noah

Moontree, you exclaim,
pointing toward the old maple
in the neighbor's yard.
We can't touch the moon,
it's too far away.
A crescent rises
through leafy branches
as we stand hand in hand,
you in your pajamas,
soft lamb clutched against your body,
face alight with wonder.

Sprite

for Winnie

I watch you in your classroom
with tiny tables, paper chains,
and a tumble of boots and mittens.
There you are, eating the lunch
your mother packed,
then finding your cubby
where your well-loved unicorn
waits to go home.
When you catch me watching
you smile and run to my arms.
Small sprite, alive with love
and laughter, stay,
stay forever in the life
we dream for you.

Atticus

We have finally reached détente.
My striped tiger cat
with thick silky fur
will not sit in my lap
or sleep next to me
on a dreary night
as cats are meant to do.
Yet he is always nearby—
underfoot when I cook,
stepping on the keyboard
and scrambling my words
until he finally curls up
in the spare desk chair
serenading me with sounds
of mouse dreams.
In return I keep fresh food in his bowl,
play a bit of flashlight tag
in the early morning,
and make myself ridiculous
by trailing a catnip mouse
around the house.
Those of us who live with cats
learn to compromise,
so, on the first cold night of winter
I was surprised
when he jumped onto the bed
and stretched out like a feline diver,
purring as he placed a paw
softly on my arm.

When My Husband Goes Away II

When my husband goes away
no music drifts
from behind his office door,
no drop-in visits to my desk,
his voice fresh with news
from the day outside.
I sit alone, searching for words
to animate the blank page,
to grasp thoughts
that swirl outside my reach,
knowing that time stretches
unmarked across the day.
The luxury of time, these hours
without intrusion,
the cruelty of solitude,
its endless reflections.

Fine China

The fine china,
nearly translucent,
hand painted with forget-me-nots
and gold-edged rims
sat in a cupboard
gathering dust.
The clothes I kept for
special occasions
were abandoned in
the back of the closet.
sagging on their stiff
wooden hangers.
But the past has become
a potpourri of memories,
and the future a hazy horizon
so, I lean into the present,
eating ordinary meals
on the blue forget-me-nots
and wearing my favorite
blue dress for a walk
around the pond.

Then and Now

We were casual about our choices
when the future lay before us,
vast and pulsing with possibility.
We played with time
and squandered our days
like penny candy,
sweet and easy to come by.

I cannot mark the moment
when time became finite,
a day as fleeting as a shooting star
darting across the winter sky,
or when I began to know
the breadth of a moment
that will not come again.

Golden Years

I imagined a time
when life's rough edges
would be smooth, and days sweet
with gratitude and remembrance.
Instead, life changes in a day,
and lapsing memory erases history.
So, we meet each other as we are,
learn to speak of death without flinching
and remind ourselves of the iridescence
of the hummingbird, hovering above
a half-empty feeder, just outside the window.

III.

COVID Days

I eat potato chips
every day at lunch
and add extra mayonnaise
to my sandwich.
My hair grows untamed
and lipstick gathers dust
on the bureau
as blank days align
like dominoes.
In the late afternoon
I eat dark chocolate
while outside wild turkeys
wander fearlessly,
bold in deserted streets.
A rusty chain secures
the playground gate
at the empty school,
and stoplights cycle
at the crosswalk,
red to green and back again.

This April

This April the daffodils
along the riverbank
bloom in rowdy profusion,
as if students in camp chairs
were sitting with legs entwined,
intoxicated by love,
as if runners were crowding
the banks, and the gaggle
of old men were sitting
on their usual bench, knee to knee.
This April the yellow blooms
sway along deserted paths,
rustling unheard in the wind,
the sound of one hand clapping.

By Chance

I met a local poet
whom I admired
quite by chance
near the bread and
poppy seed bagels.
We chatted through our masks
about the difficulty of writing
during a pandemic,
about a poet's habit
of collecting fragments
for some future creation,
and about where we
might be buried.
It felt oddly natural
talking about death
with someone I barely knew,
while grocery carts
wheeled past and
the register rang up
a Tuscan sandwich
with mozzarella
and prosciutto.

Quarantine

I have grown accustomed
to the quiet, our senses quickened,
alert to the sound of leaves
in warm summer wind,
the clicking of a sprinkler
tilting toward dry grass,
neighbors' voices muffled by masks.
I move through familiar rooms
where sunlight falls across a faded chair,
its silent warmth a solace.
It has been a comfort, this quiet,
soothing me like a fog,
blurring the sharp outlines
of despair.

Birds

I haven't heard them before,
the birds whose morning song
cascades through still air
as they gather
on backyard branches.
Maybe they are newcomers
lured by the empty streets
and budding trees
of a moribund city,
or was I deaf to birdsong,
smothered by shrill voices,
wailing sirens,
the drone of airplanes
with crisscrossing vapor trails.

Love Story

The first snow falls early,
sealing us in our house of quarantine.
I once feared the loneliness of two,
but we have traveled together
beyond the dictates of hurried days,
eating oranges you cut into curving bites,
and dinners invented from a thinning larder.
In the quiet evening we find each other,
speaking a language born of years.
It is enough, this reacquaintance,
this sanctuary, it is more than enough.

IV.

Morning Light

In a room with morning light
orchids bloomed then faded
and a computer screen
displayed documents
with changes tracked.
A coffee mug with a lipstick imprint
sat beside paper clips
and a battered stapler,
the clutter of office life,
my second skin.

In that room the hours were
locked into an architecture
of meetings, tasks named
and completed,
lives shared over lukewarm coffee,
a baby's fever, a new love,
a marriage unraveling,
the shape of days.

I once yearned for that morning light
and the orchids in bloom,
but now I dive deep
into remembrance,
striving to place words on paper,
scrappy stars in a paper galaxy
all my own.

Two Poems

I read a poem
I had always
wanted to write,
about driving north
in late spring
and finding spring again,
pendulous lilacs
now spent in my city garden,
so full of bloom
their branches bend
to the ground.
But in my poem
there is a robin's nest
just outside the window
where a mother bird
sits atop her clutch,
three blue eggs,
small, speckled
and almost perfect.

Night Swim

for Heather and Susie

We swam at night
under the desert sky,
our voices lifting
into the dark
while tendrils of steam
rose from the pool,
disappearing into dry air.
In the tepid water we found
an easy intimacy,
an unspoken promise.
The constellations,
winter brilliant,
shone through the clear sky,
bright and unchanging.

A Thousand Words

It is not true that the Inuit have
a thousand words for snow
as I have always heard,
but surely their thirty or forty will do.
I don't know how many words
the Inuit have for love,
but my guess is it's more than one.
Here, where English is spoken,
love is overburdened.
We know the love that kindles ecstasy
and the agony of heartbreak,
the love of a child that awakens devotion
deep and unbounded,
and the love of a god,
with its cloak of adoration.
How well we know the ways
love carves its history
on the contours of our souls.

Faith

I do not believe in the god
I knew as a child,
kind and all-knowing.
In a world where men
shatter what is sacred,
and children languish
forgotten at borders,
faith eludes me.
Yet sometimes I pray,
to whom or to what
I don't always know,
but in the moment
a snowflake's perfect prism
hardens on winter glass,
or a child folds his small body
into yours, surely
we know the divine.

Red Line

Beneath the city
we are a strange brotherhood,
detached from the crumpled ice
and skidding cars on the streets.
The train rattles noisily along
while we sit side by side,
a young girl on my right
texting with both thumbs,
her nails a polished cerise.
To my left a man
in construction boots
and a worn canvas jacket
holds his empty lunch pail,
head tilted back, eyes closed.
I read the overhead posters
advertising night schools
and medical trials,
others study the grimy subway floor
or look toward dark windows
that reflect our small company,
its singular intimacy
lasting only a stop or two.

Matinee

In the movie house
the old woman's bent torso
is backlit against the screen
as she moves toward her seat,
while he, tall and stooped
walks behind her
carrying their popcorn
with a trembling hand.
They settle into velveteen chairs
whispering to each other
in the dimming light,
arranging their coats carefully
behind them.
When the movie begins
we look to the screen,
neatly ordered, obedient
in our geometry and silence,
trading a dreary winter afternoon
for intrigue and technicolor.

Drinking

He wanders
in a wilderness
of grief, retreating
to the bottle,
then returns
for a day or two
to speak about
the son he lost,
the pain that does not
diminish with time,
and his despair.
He flees again,
drinking vodka
poorly disguised
in a water bottle,
pints stashed
behind the daylilies,
and in the branch
of the crooked maple.
We try to reach
across the chasm
of his suffering, but he is
far beyond our touch,
wrapped in a shroud
of memories.

Cardinal

*It turns out
that the red cardinal
in the green pine tree
is important,*
you tell me.
There is a number
none of us knows,
maybe months
or even weeks.
We speak about
early spring light,
our children becoming parents,
the tree you have chosen
for your ashes,
and other things
that matter.

Graveside

The day was soft and warm,
alive with early spring.
Your favorite horse
pulled your casket up the stony hill
where we lifted the pine box
onto the wide strapping
above your grave.

We spoke in turn, benign words
about bravery and loss,
but in the unspoken etiquette of death
we did not reveal the moments
when you demanded
more than we could give,
or when your anger flashed,
scalding those you loved.

When the eulogies were finished
we reached into the warm black soil,
fragrant with decay
from so many seasons
beneath the apple tree,
and placed a handful
in your grave,
as if to say goodbye.

Mountain Lake

An old villa sits empty
on the shore, sad and disused,
its overgrown gardens
reclaiming the once manicured lawn.
Along the broad veranda
vines twist through the portico
wrapping tapered columns
in woody stems.
Diving into the lake
I shatter its reflection
into droplets, and float
on the crystalline water
as light as balsa,
weightless and in awe.

At the Dock

Three windows look
toward the harbor,
their blinds covered in grime
and salt spray, hanging askew.
Chairs with tattered cushions
lean against the far wall
where fishermen gather
around an old wood stove.
On the wall near the scale
a series of small pencil drawings
from a spiral pad hang
from yellowing tape.
Captains with winter beards
and knitted caps,
cocky young sternmen
with cigarettes dangling,
and this year a woman
with braided hair and
a slightly slanted smile.

Fog

In the fog
at night
every direction
seems right,
which is how
we got lost
on calm black water,
daylight fading into evening
and buoys floating atop
their own reflections.
When trees emerged
they were the wrong trees,
so we turned
with the quiet lapping of water
to guide us.
Losing sight of land,
of familiar markers,
we saw only thick air,
grey and wet,
until a prick of light
refracting through the fog
guided us past boats
moored in the silent harbor,
to the ghost dock
where slowly our island
emerged from the
darkening evening
like Brigadoon,
like home.

Roses

Sometimes cutting the stems
and adding warm water
revives the roses,
but not usually. More often
they continue to fade,
drooping slightly
then browning at the edges
as they unfold,
petals drying to paper
and falling to the table.
These days I keep the flowers
until they drop,
admiring the beauty
in the slow draining of life.

Summer's End

Children's voices
no longer fill the house,
quiet has settled in.
Towering clouds of autumn
gather in billows
over the mountains,
the blue heron
has returned,
resting on one leg
in the shallows,
and the garden spiders
spin webs that catch
the autumn light.
Fall descends softly,
the sweet warmth
of summer lingering
until the equinox,
when day and night align
in perfect symmetry
before tipping toward the dark.

About the Author

Emily H. Axelrod has published two previous books of poems, *Passerby* (Antrim House, 2015), and *North Window* (Finishing Line Press, 2020). Her work has been published in the *Muddy River Review, the Galway Review, the Café Review,* and the online literary site, *On the Seawall*. Ms. Axelrod's poems are influenced by a professional background in urban placemaking, a California childhood, and family life. She lives and works in Cambridge, MA.

www.ingramcontent.com/pod-product-compliance
Lightning Source LLC
Chambersburg PA
CBHW031118160426
43193CB00031B/514